The Angel And Mary

1 = blue   2 = yellow   3 = red   4 = brown   5 = purple   6 = green
9 = black   10 = tan   11 = orange   blank spots = you pick

Joseph's Dream

Matthew 1:20-21

1 = blue   2 = yellow   3 = red   4 = brown   5 = purple
8 = gray   10 = tan   11 = orange   blank spots = you pick

2

A Long Trip

Luke 2:4

1 = blue   2 = yellow   3 = red   4 = brown   5 = purple   6 = green
7 = pink   8 = gray   9 = black   10 = tan   11 = orange
blank spots = you pick

No Room

Luke 2:7

1 = blue   2 = yellow   3 = red   4 = brown   5 = purple   6 = green
8 = gray   9 = black   10 = tan   11 = orange   blank spots = you pick

Jesus Is Born

Luke 2:6-7

1 = blue   2 = yellow   3 = red   4 = brown   5 = purple
8 = gray   9 = black   10 = tan   11 = orange   blank spots = you pick

Shepherds In The Fields

Luke 2:8

1 = blue   2 = yellow   3 = red   4 = brown   5 = purple   6 = green
8 = gray   9 = black   10 = tan   11 = orange   blank spots = you pick

Watching Their Sheep

Luke 2:8

2 = yellow   3 = red   4 = brown   5 = purple   6 = green   8 = gray
9 = black   10 = tan   blank spots = you pick

Angel Appears

Luke 2:9

1 = blue   2 = yellow   4 = brown   5 = purple   6 = green
8 = gray   9 = black   10 = tan   11 = orange   blank spots = you pick

Good News

Luke 2:9-10

1 = blue   2 = yellow   3 = red   4 = brown   5 = purple   6 = green
8 = gray   9 = black   10 = tan   11 = orange   blank spots = you pick

A Baby Wrapped In Cloths

Luke 2:7

1 = blue   2 = yellow   3 = red   4 = brown   5 = purple   6 = green
7 = pink   8 = gray   9 = black   10 = tan   11 = orange
blank spots = you pick

Glory To God

Luke 2:13-14

2 = yellow   3 = red   4 = brown   5 = purple   6 = green   8 = gray
9 = black   11 = orange   blank spots = you pick

Let's Go To Bethlehem

Luke 2:15

1 = blue   2 = yellow   3 = red   4 = brown   5 = purple   6 = green
8 = gray   9 = black   10 = tan   11 = orange   blank spots = you pick

Lying In A Manger

Luke 2:16

1 = blue   2 = yellow   3 = red   4 = brown   5 = purple   8 = gray
9 = black   10 = tan   11 = orange   blank spots = you pick

Mary And Jesus

Luke 2:6–7

1 = blue   2 = yellow   3 = red   5 = purple   7 = pink   9 = black
10 = tan   blank spots = you pick

Magi From The East

Matthew 2:1-2

1 = blue   2 = yellow   3 = red   4 = brown   5 = purple   6 = green
7 = pink   8 = gray   9 = black   10 = tan   11 = orange
blank spots = you pick

15

Magi Follow The Star

Matthew 2:9-10

1 = blue   2 = yellow   4 = brown   5 = purple   6 = green
8 = gray   9 = black   10 = tan   11 = orange   blank spots = you pick

16

They Worshiped Jesus

Matthew 2:11

1 = blue **2** = yellow **3** = red **4** = brown **5** = purple **6** = green
7 = pink **8** = gray **9** = black **10** = tan **11** = orange
blank spots = you pick

Special Gifts

Matthew 2:11

1 = blue   2 = yellow   3 = red   4 = brown   5 = purple   6 = green
7 = pink   8 = gray   9 = black   10 = tan   11 = orange
blank spots = you pick

18

Town Of Bethlehem

2 = yellow   4 = brown   6 = green   8 = gray   9 = black   10 = tan
11 = orange   blank spots = you pick

Baby Jesus

2 = yellow   3 = red   4 = brown   5 = purple   7 = pink   8 = gray
9 = black   10 = tan   blank spots = you pick

Festive Ornaments

1 = blue   2 = yellow   3 = red   5 = purple   6 = green   7 = pink
11 = orange   blank spots = you pick

Celebration Goodies

1 = blue   2 = yellow   3 = red   4 = brown   5 = purple   6 = green
7 = pink   10 = tan   11 = orange   blank spots = you pick

Sparkling Tree

1 = blue   2 = yellow   3 = red   4 = brown   5 = purple   6 = green
7 = pink   8 = gray   11 = orange   blank spots = you pick

Wonderful Wreath

1 = blue   2 = yellow   3 = red   5 = purple   6 = green   7 = pink
8 = gray   11 = orange   blank spots = you pick

Magi Crown

1 = blue   2 = yellow   3 = red   5 = purple   6 = green   7 = pink
8 = gray   11 = orange   blank spots = you pick

How Many Can You Find?

How many of each can you find in the box below?

Answers: chicken: 5, gold: 3, camel: 5, pig: 7, star: 9, crown: 5, wise men: 4, Baby Jesus: 3, bird: 3, horse: 2

How Many Can You Find?

How many of each can you find in the box below?

___ 🐰 ___ 🐑 ___ 🐭 ___ 🐄 ___ 🧍
___ 👼 ___ 🏺 ___ 🛖 ___ 👬 ___ 🌃

Answers: bunny: 6, sheep: 8, mouse: 4, cow: 9, Joseph: 3, angel: 6, myrrh: 3, manger: 5, shepherds: 5, Bethlehem: 6

Spot The Difference

Can you find 10 differences in the pictures below?

1. Bow on wreath 2. Book 3. Cat's hat 4. Dog's collar 5. Holly on lamp 6. Candle in lamp 7. Music note 8. Girl's mitten 9. Steps 10. Tree in background

Spot The Difference

Can you find 10 differences in the pictures below?

1. Cookie cutter 2. Pictures on fridge 3. Magnets 4. Girl's hairclips 5. Cookie on tray 6. Cookie jar 7. Dog's tongue 8. Lines on measuring cup 9. Mixing bowl 10. Grandma's glasses

Joseph And Mary Travel To Bethlehem

Caesar Augustus made a law that everyone needed to return to their hometown to be counted. So Joseph and Mary traveled to the town of Bethlehem. Help Joseph and Mary get to Bethlehem.

start

end

No Place To Stay

When Joseph and Mary arrived in Bethlehem, there were no rooms available. A kind innkeeper said they could stay in his stable with the animals. Help Joseph and Mary get to the stable.

start ▽

end

The Shepherds Go To Bethlehem

Help the shepherds get to Bethlehem to see baby Jesus.

start ▷

end

When the angels had left them and gone into heaven, the shepherds said to one another, "Let's go to Bethlehem and see this thing that has happened, which the Lord has told us about." So they hurried off and found Mary and Joseph, and the baby, who was lying in the manger. When they had seen him, they spread the word concerning what had been told them about this child, and all who heard it were amazed at what the shepherds said to them. Luke 2:15–18 NIV

The Wise Men Follow The Star

Help the wise men follow the star to present Jesus with gifts of gold, frankincense, and myrrh.

start

end

When they saw the star, they were overjoyed. On coming to the house, they saw the child with his mother Mary, and they bowed down and worshiped him. Then they opened their treasures and presented him with gifts of gold, frankincense and myrrh. Matthew 2:10–11 NIV

Jesus' Family Escapes To Egypt

When they had gone, an angel of the Lord appeared to Joseph in a dream. "Get up," he said, "take the child and his mother and escape to Egypt. Stay there until I tell you, for Herod is going to search for the child to kill him." So he got up, took the child and his mother during the night and left for Egypt. Matthew 2:13–14 NIV.

Help Joseph, Mary, and Jesus get to Egypt.

start

end

Luke 1:37

Use the code below to find out what Gabriel said about God.

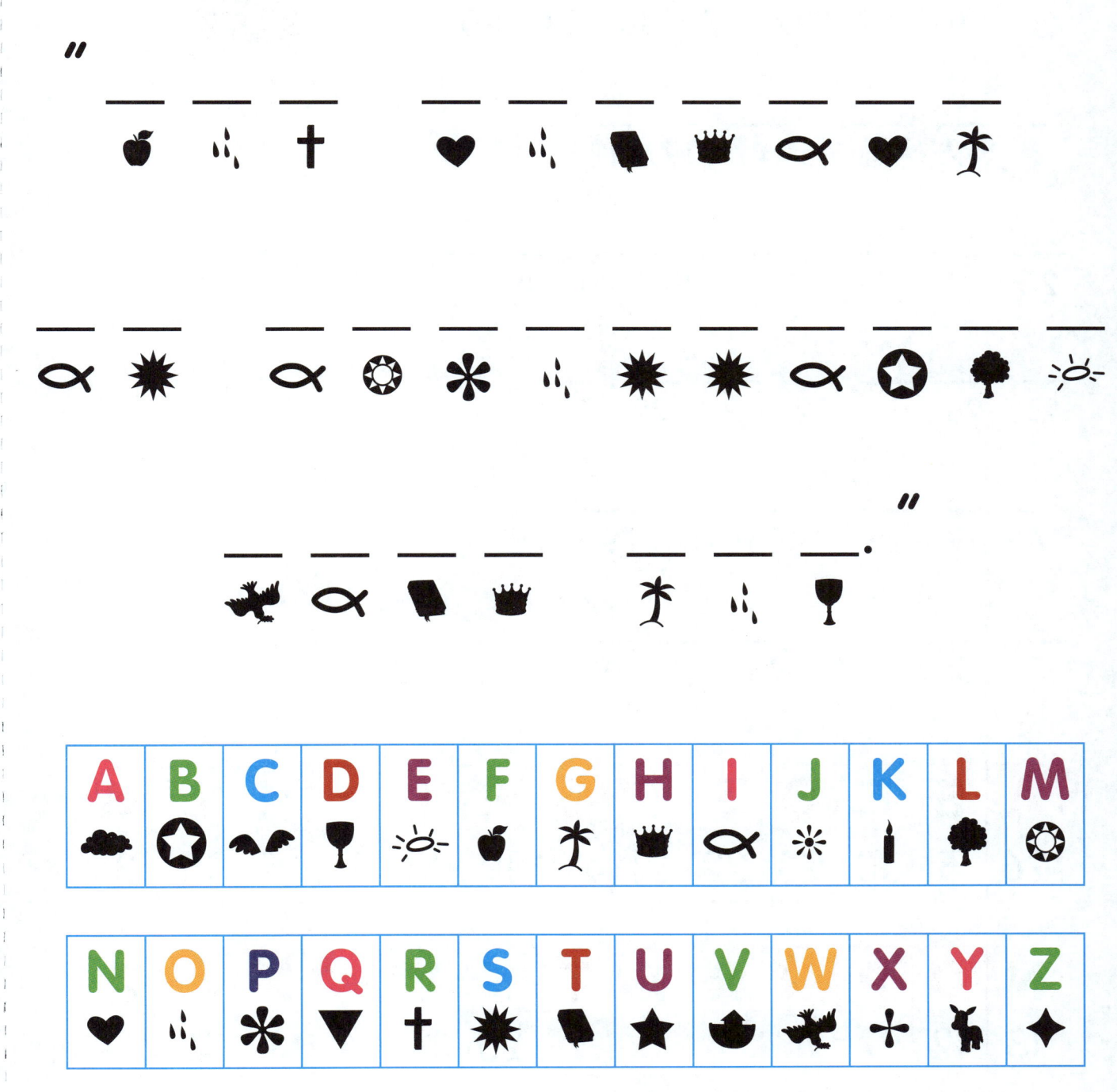

Answer: "For nothing is impossible with God."

Gabriel Visits Mary

Use the code below to find out what the angel Gabriel said to Mary.

"__ __ __ __ __ __ __ __ __,
  20 9 22 22 7 18 13 20 8

__ __ __   __ __ __
 2 12 25   4 19 12

__ __ __   __ __ __ __ __ __
26 9 22 19 18 20 19 15 2

__ __ __ __ __ __ __!
21 26 14 12 9 22 23

__ __ __   __ __ __ __
 7 19 22 15 12 9 23

__ __   __ __ __ __   __ __ __."
18 8   4 18 7 19   2 12 25

A	B	C	D	E	F	G	H	I	J	K	L	M
26	5	10	23	22	21	20	19	18	11	6	15	3

N	O	P	Q	R	S	T	U	V	W	X	Y	Z
13	12	17	16	9	8	7	25	14	4	1	2	24

Answer: "Greetings, you who are highly favored! The Lord is with you."

Mary Praises God

Use the code below to find out what Mary says. Luke 1:46–47 ICB

"

$\overline{3}$ $\overline{2}$ $\overline{8}$ $\overline{12}$ $\overline{25}$ $\overline{15}$

$\overline{17}$ $\overline{9}$ $\overline{26}$ $\overline{18}$ $\overline{8}$ $\overline{22}$ $\overline{8}$ $\overline{7}$ $\overline{19}$ $\overline{22}$

$\overline{15}$ $\overline{12}$ $\overline{9}$ $\overline{23}$; $\overline{3}$ $\overline{2}$ $\overline{19}$ $\overline{22}$ $\overline{26}$ $\overline{9}$ $\overline{7}$

$\overline{18}$ $\overline{8}$ $\overline{19}$ $\overline{26}$ $\overline{17}$ $\overline{17}$ $\overline{2}$

$\overline{5}$ $\overline{22}$ $\overline{10}$ $\overline{26}$ $\overline{25}$ $\overline{8}$ $\overline{22}$ $\overline{20}$ $\overline{12}$ $\overline{23}$ $\overline{18}$ $\overline{8}$

$\overline{3}$ $\overline{2}$ $\overline{8}$ $\overline{26}$ $\overline{14}$ $\overline{18}$ $\overline{12}$ $\overline{9}$. "

A	B	C	D	E	F	G	H	I	J	K	L	M
26	5	10	23	22	21	20	19	18	11	6	15	3

N	O	P	Q	R	S	T	U	V	W	X	Y	Z
13	12	17	16	9	8	7	25	14	4	1	2	24

Answer: "My soul praises the Lord; my heart is happy because God is my Savior."

37

Joseph's Dream

Use the code below to find out what the angel told Joseph in a dream.

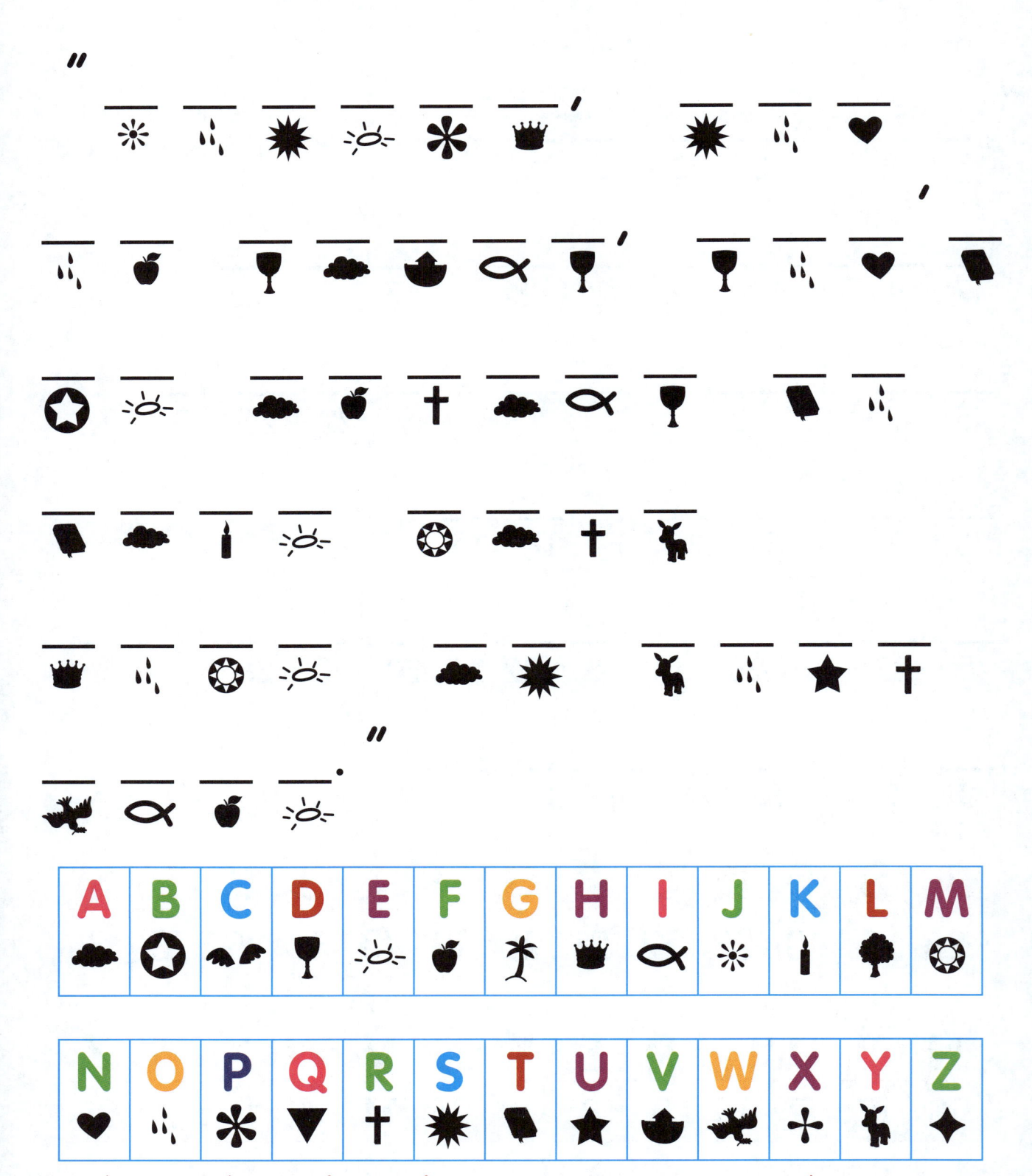

"_ _ _ _ _ _ _,   _ _ _ _

_ _   _ _ _ _ _ _ _,   _ _ _ _ _

_ _   _ _ _ _ _ _ _ _ _ _

_ _ _ _   _ _ _ _ _ _ _

_ _ _ _   _ _   _ _ _ _ _   _ _ _ _

_ _ _ _ ."

A	B	C	D	E	F	G	H	I	J	K	L	M

N	O	P	Q	R	S	T	U	V	W	X	Y	Z

Answer: "Joseph, son of David, don't be afraid to take Mary home as your wife." (Matthew 1:20)

Good News of Great Joy

Use the code below to find out what the angel says to the shepherds about Jesus' birth.

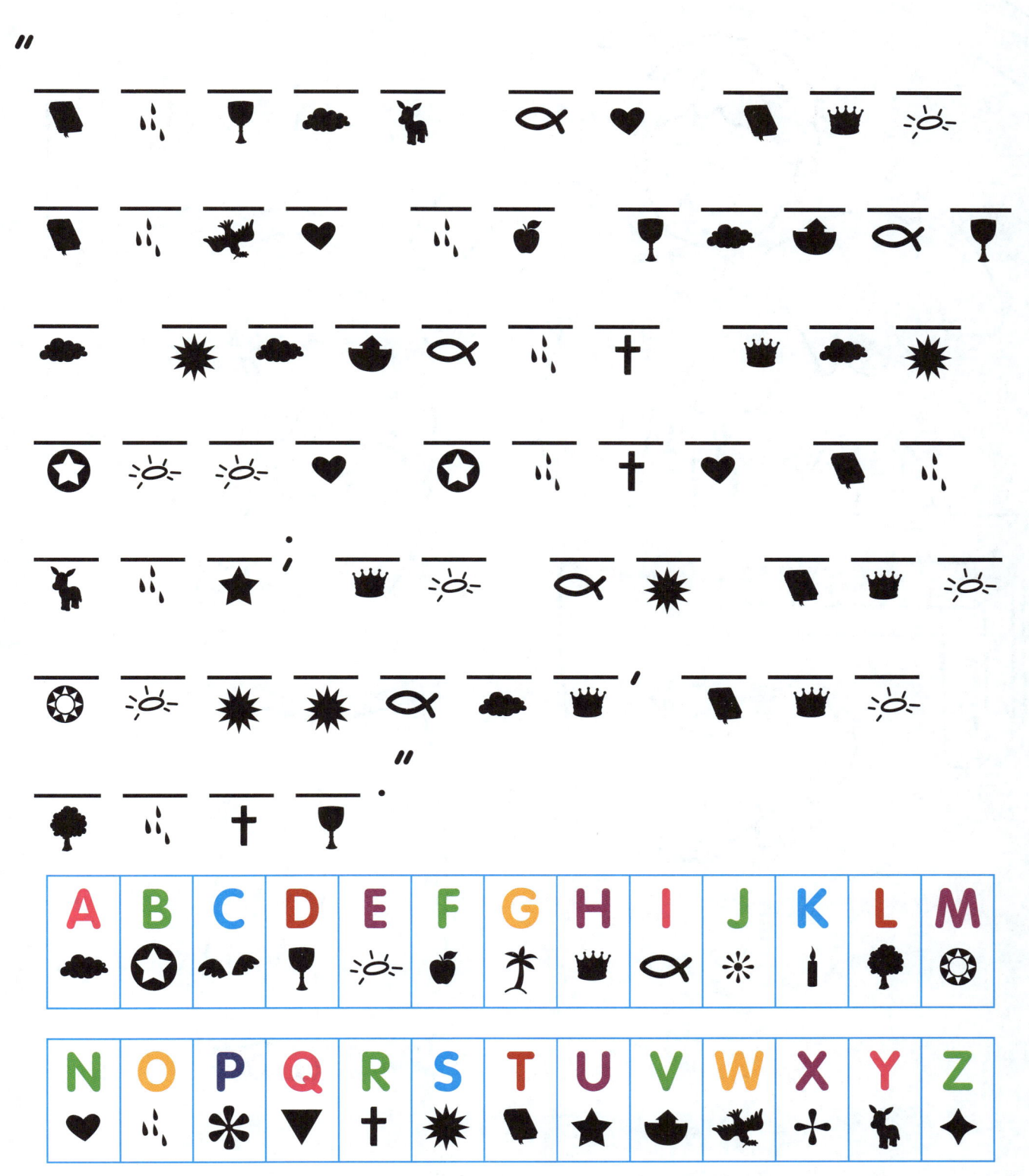

"_ _ _ _ _ _ _ _ _ _
 _ _ _ _ _ _ _ _ _ _ _ _
 _ _ _ _ _ _ _ _ _ _
 _ _ _ _ _ _ _ _ _ _
 _ _ _ ; _ _ _ _ _ _ _ _ _
 _ _ _ _ _ _ _ _ ' _ _ _ _ ."
 _ _ _ _ .

A	B	C	D	E	F	G	H	I	J	K	L	M

N	O	P	Q	R	S	T	U	V	W	X	Y	Z

Answer: "Today in the town of David a Savior has been born to you; he is the Messiah, the Lord." Luke 2:11 NIV

Luke 1:30–31

"Do not be afraid, Mary; you have found favor with God. You will conceive and give birth to a son, and you are to call him Jesus."

Matthew 1:20–21

An angel of the Lord appeared to him in a dream and said, "Joseph son of David, do not be afraid to take Mary home as your wife, because what is conceived in her is from the Holy Spirit. She will give birth to a son, and you are to give him the name Jesus, because he will save his people from their sins."

Luke 2:4–5

So Joseph also went up from the town of Nazareth in Galilee to Judea, to Bethlehem the town of David, because he belonged to the house and line of David. He went there to register with Mary, who was pledged to be married to him and was expecting a child.

No Room

Luke 2:7
There was no guest room available for them.

Luke 2:6–7

While they were there, the time came for the baby to be born, and she gave birth to her firstborn, a son. She wrapped him in cloths and placed him in a manger.

Luke 2:8

There were shepherds living out in the fields nearby…

Luke 2:9

An angel of the Lord appeared to the shepherds.

Luke 2:13–14

Suddenly a great company of the heavenly host appeared with the angel, praising God and saying, "Glory to God in the highest heaven, and on earth peace to those on whom his favor rests."

Luke 2:15–16

When the angels had left them and gone into heaven, the shepherds said to one another, "Let's go to Bethlehem and see this thing that has happened, which the Lord has told us about." So they hurried off and found Mary and Joseph, and the baby, who was lying in the manger.